Hide & Seek with Evil

Written by
Sergiu Troaca

Illustrated by
Tu Minh Hoang

This book is based on a true story as told by the subject.

We strive for accuracy but if you see something that doesn't look right, contact us at infoabookbyme@gmail.com.

Hide & Seek With Evil - Eva & Anne
Copyright © Never Forget Publishing 2016

Special thanks to the student designers at Augustana College and particularly to Jasen Hengst for his focus on developing a brand image that is consistent with our mission.

All rights reserved. No part of this publication may be reproduced or stored in a retrieval system or transmitted in any form or by any means – electronic, mechanical, digital, photocopy, recording or any other means – except for brief quotations in printed revisions, without prior permission of the author and publisher.

A BOOK by
Holocaust Series

History comes alive with true stories written by children for children

NEVER FORGET PUBLISHING

A BOOK by ME is dedicated to the Quad Cities' Three Esthers

Esther Avruch   **Esther Katz**   **Esther Schiff**

Also, lovingly dedicated to Ida Kramer, Holocaust Historian, & Edith Levy, Jewish Holocaust Survivor & Author

MISSION STATEMENT:
A BOOK by ME® seeks to preserve the history of the Holocaust and other human rights issues. Our desire is to preserve the stories for the next generation so lessons of tolerance, empathy, hope and respect are not lost.

Deb Bowen's work with young authors is important for our generation and the next. Without her, some stories may have gotten lost. Her work is geared towards realization and understanding, hence, prevention. I fully believe in the importance of her work for generations to come.

Dr. Edith Rechter Levy, Ph.D
Holocaust Survivor, Author and Scholar

Dear Reader,

    My name is Sergiu Troaca, and I'm from Romania. I came to the United States as an exchange student living in the Midwest during the school year of 2007-08. My host mom is Deb Bowen, Creator of A BOOK by ME. I heard Eva Schloss speak at Yom Hashoah and was excited to write about her story. I hope you enjoy learning about her.

Name:	Eva Geiringer
Born:	May 11, 1929 in Vienna, Austria
Family:	Parents, Erich and Elfriede, and a brother Heinz
Story:	Eva's father took his family to Holland in hopes they would be safe from Hitler. There, they met other families who were hiding from the Nazis as well. One young lady who lived across the courtyard was Anne Frank. Read how Anne and Eva ended up playing hide and seek from the Nazis.

Eva Geiringer

    I admire Eva so much for speaking about her suffering. It was very interesting to hear about her story and her mother's life after the war when she married Otto Frank.

    If you want to do something awesome, become a young author or illustrator through A BOOK by ME. I'm glad I did and you will be too!

Best Wishes,
Sergiu Troaca
Romania

During World War II, two eleven-year-old girls and their families moved to the same street in Amsterdam. Because they were Jewish, their parents thought they had a better chance for safety in Holland. Anne Frank lived in an apartment with her parents and her older sister, and Eva Geiringer lived with her parents and her older brother.

Anne was mostly interested in clothes and fashion like her sister, while Eva was more of a tomboy. The girls enjoyed playing board games together. As the Nazi party moved into Holland, they took away their rights to go to restaurants or to movies.

Both girls wanted to see the movie *Snow White*, a new American film released by Walt Disney, but they didn't have that freedom. Jews were not allowed in theaters after the Nazis came.

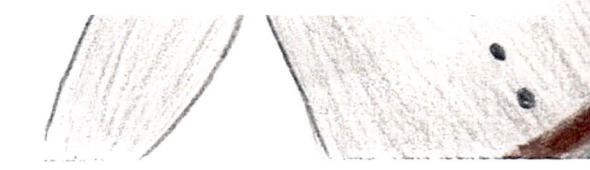

A horrible man by the name of Adolf Hitler founded the Nazi party which had taken over Germany and many other countries in Europe.

Hitler believed the Jewish people had no freedoms or rights. Both fathers hoped to keep their families safe by moving to the Netherlands, but the Nazis invaded. They were no longer safe.

The Jewish families tried to live their lives normally, but life was now shadowed with fear. One day, the soldiers told Eva's family they could no longer own a row boat. Jewish people were no longer free to own a car or a boat or a bicycle.

Because they were Jews, it was obvious they were not going to be able to live in safety, so both fathers decided to hide their families.

Anne and her family hid in her father's office building. A good friend brought them food and supplies because they did not dare go outside for fear they would be discovered.

For two years, they lived this horrible game of hide and seek from the Nazis. Anne passed the time by writing in her diary.

Eva's father decided to split up his family so they would have a better chance of survival. He found two hiding places, so Eva hid with her mother in a small room at a friend's house, while her brother hid with their father.

It frightened young Eva to be separated from her father and brother. She wanted the family to stay together, but it was not her decision.

Sadly, all three hiding places were discovered by the Nazis. Anne and Eva, along with their families, were taken to prison camps set up for the Jewish people.

All their belongings were taken away from them. They were not given enough food, supplies or medication. Many innocent people died because of the terrible conditions in the concentration camps.

The horrible camp was called Auschwitz, and the men and women were housed in separate barracks. Eva was very thankful to be with her mother. It was a miracle they both survived the camp.

When the Russian soldiers came to rescue them, Eva and her mother discovered her father and brother had died. Her friend Anne, Anne's sister, and Anne's mother also died in the prison camp. Otto, Anne's father, was the only survivor in their family.

Once free of the prison camp, Anne's father came to Eva and her mother after the war. He brought Anne's diary with him. He asked if they thought he should publish it.

Eva, her mother, and Otto all agreed. Anne's diary must be read by people from all over the world to help them understand the suffering of the Jewish people during this horrible war.

Otto Frank fell in love with Eva's mother and they married. Together, they traveled the world sharing Anne's diary and telling their own stories of survival.

From the Family Album

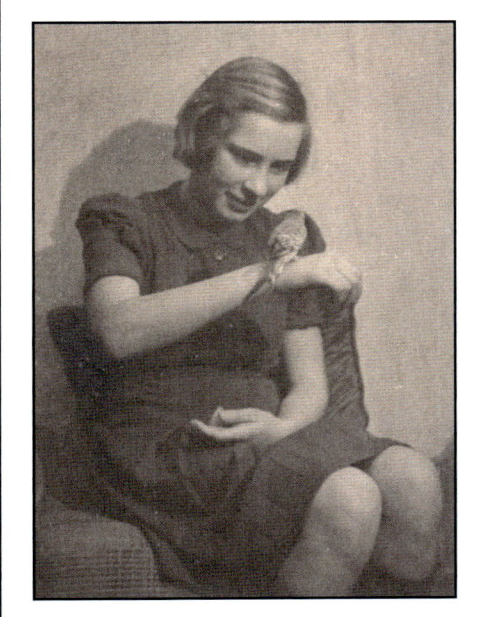

Eva as a child

Eva's brother Heinz

Eva as a young woman

Eva and Deb Bowen,
Creator A BOOK by ME

. Eva and Ida Kramer,
Quad Cities Holocaust Historian

Eva with Cassie Bowen
(Curriculum Development for A
BOOK by ME) and Deb Bowen

Eva Geiringer Schloss
Jewish Holocaust Survivor

I was born in 1929 to a wonderful Jewish family in Vienna, Austria. I had a brother, Heinz, who was three years older than me. As World War II heated up throughout Europe, we were not safe, so we immigrated to Belgium and eventually to Amsterdam, the capital city of The Netherlands, in 1940. This was two years after Hitler annexed Austria. In early 1938, Nazi Germany seized Austria by force to add the nation to the German Reich, or empire.

It was during this time that we first met the Frank family. They had moved to Amsterdam for the same reason. When the Germans invaded The Netherlands in 1942, our family went into hiding. In May 1944, we were betrayed, captured by the Nazis, and sent to the Auschwitz-Birkenau death camp.

Most prisoners sent to that camp were killed because the Nazis wanted to murder all the Jews, as well as other minority groups. My mother and I were lucky to survive, and we were liberated in January 1945 by Russian soldiers. They shared their soup and bread with us. I was very moved by their kindness, and my emotions got the better of me. They didn't realize their kind human act would touch me so.

As fighting was still going on in the west, we were evacuated eastward deep into Russia. Eventually, in June 1945, we were returned to Amsterdam, where we heard the devastating news that my father and brother had not survived.

Otto Frank had also returned from Auschwitz and came to see us. He told us the terrible news that his whole family had died. A few days later, he came again with a little parcel under his arm. He opened it very carefully. I remember it very clearly; it was Anne's diary.

I felt it was a lifeline for him because he was in a desperate state. Through the diary, he felt that Anne was still with him. He made it his task to publish it and promote her story. He came very often to visit us. He helped mother with me. I was a very sad, difficult teenager, full of hatred and suspicion and couldn't make friends. He was a childless father, a man who had lost both his children. Through our pain, we became extremely close.

Otto persuaded my mother that I should return to school, so I resumed my education. I studied art history at Amsterdam University. From there, I went to London to train as a professional photographer for a year. During that time, my mom and Otto became even closer.

In London, I met Zvi Schloss, a young man from Israel, and we got married in 1952. My mother and Otto were married the next year. They were together for 27 years, and I've never seen a happier marriage. They devoted their lives to working with Anne's diary. When it was eventually translated into seventy languages, they answered thousands of letters from all over the world. When my mother died, I found copies of 30,000 letters. This really was the focus of their lives.

Today, Zvi and I live in London and have three daughters and five grandchildren. From 1972 until 1997, I ran an antiques shop in Edgware, a district of London. Since 1985, I have become increasingly active in Holocaust education and felt privileged to receive an Honorary Doctorate in Civil Law from the University of Northumbria in Newcastle, England. I also became a Trustee of the Anne Frank Educational Trust, United Kingdom.

In 1988, my autobiography, *Eva's Story,* was published, providing an opportunity for people to read about my life. In 1995, I cooperated with playwright James Still in the creation of the educational play *And Then They Came for Me: Remembering the World of Anne Frank,* about four teenagers during the Holocaust. The play has been widely performed, and I have had the honor of sharing my experiences in cities across the U.S., England, Europe, and Australia. In 2005, I wrote *The Promise,* a children's book about my life, with Barbara Powers, an educator from Chicago, Illinois. In 2013, I released my third book, titled *After Auschwitz.* My books are available at amazon.com.

Otto Frank with Eva, her children and her mother in the flower garden.
(Photo taken many years after the war.)

"Once I really am in power, my first and foremost task will be the annihilation of the Jews." * -Adolf Hitler
*Hitler's words in 1922, according to Major Josef Hell, a German journalist in the 20s and 30s

About the Author
Sergiu Troaca

Author Sergiu Troaca is an exchange student from Romania who spent ten months in the U.S. at Aledo High School in Aledo, Illinois in 2008. Sergiu enjoyed participating in the exchange, especially experiencing American restaurants, Six Flags theme park and Branson, Missouri.

His friendship with Quad Cities Holocaust Expert Ida Kramer led him to hear speaker Eva Schloss at a Holocaust Remembrance ceremony. Her story of survival impacted his life, so he became a young author writing Eva's story for younger readers.

Author Sergiu Troaca, Ida Kramer (Holocaust Historian) and Author Barbara Scholzen (*Jolanta and Her 2,500 Kids*)

Romania borders the Black Sea, Bulgaria, Ukraine, Hungary, Serbia, and Moldova. With 19.94 million inhabitants, the country is the seventh most populous member state of the European Union (EU). Its capital and largest city, Bucharest, is the sixth largest city in the EU.

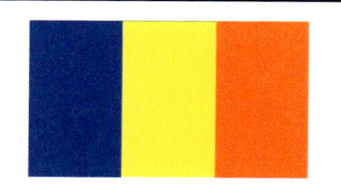

About the Illustrator
Tu Minh Hoang

Illustrator Tu Minh Hoang (nickname Bi) is an exchange student from Vietnam who enjoyed attending Westmer High School in Joy, Illinois. Her art teacher at the school was a great source of inspiration as Bi worked on drawings of young Eva and Anne Frank.

Deb Bowen, A BOOK by ME with Bi Hoang in Des Moines, Iowa

Vietnam is the easternmost country in Southeast Asia. It is bordered by China to the north, Laos to the northwest, Cambodia to the southwest, and Malaysia across the sea to the southeast. The capital city is Hanoi.

Holocaust Series Book 7

LEARNING STATION

Vocabulary and Key Terms

Adolf Hitler – the leader of the National Socialist German Workers' (Nazi) Party and leader of Germany during the time of World War II

Allied Powers – countries (Great Britain, France, Russia, United States) and other smaller countries who fought against Germany, Italy and Japan during World War II

Auschwitz – the largest of the German concentration camps located in Poland; a guarded confinement where prisoners are forced to work

barrack – a large, dreary building used for lodging many people

concentration camp – a guarded confinement where prisoners are forced to work

Holocaust – the killing of six million European Jews and millions of other selected groups during World War II (also known as The Shoah)

Jew – an ethnic and religious group of people

Nazi – a member of a political party called National Socialist German Workers' Party, led by Adolf Hitler

survival – the act of living, usually while enduring a traumatic or dangerous event

World War II – a war that took place primarily in Europe that began in 1939 and ended in 1945 involving all of the world's powers and other smaller nations

Short Summary

Teenager Eva and her brother Heinz moved with their parents to a new country called Holland to live. Even though they were trying to stay safe, they soon had to go into hiding from the Nazis. They hid in three different places. Anne Frank's family also went into hiding. The hiding places were found by the Nazis and the families were taken to Auschwitz. Read about Eva's survival.

MLA Citation

Troaca, Sergiu. *Hide & Seek with Evil*. Vol. 7. Ill. Hoang, Tu. Aledo, IL: Never Forget, 2016. Print. Holocaust Ser.

Topics Covered

Anti-Bullying
Anti-Semitism
Bravery
Holocaust
Survival
WWII History

©Never Forget Publishing

Holocaust Series Book 7

LEARNING STATION

Thinking Strategies

- Making Connections – Connect the reading to the existing schema.
- Questioning – Question before, during, and after reading. Consider the content, ideas, and events.
- Visualizing – Use background knowledge, make mental pictures of the text.
- Inferring – Use knowledge to infer the underlying theme or idea to interpret meaning.
- Determining Importance – Develop summarizing skills.
- Synthesizing – Make sense of important information to construct deeper meaning.

Pre-Reading Activity

Anne Frank's received a red and white checkered diary for her 13th birthday. When her family had to go into hiding from the Nazis in 1942, Anne took her diary with her and wrote about her thoughts and feelings while living in hiding. After the war, her father, Otto, compiled her diary into a book called *Anne Frank: The Diary of a Young Girl*. Have students read three or four entries from Anne's diary to get to know her. This will help give the students background knowledge of the setting and culture of the World War II era and insight on Anne's personality. In this way, the students will learn about both main characters before they read about Eva and her friend, Anne, in *Hide & Seek with Evil*.

Related Literature & Media

A BOOK by ME Holocaust Series *
- Book #17 *Never Lose Hope* is about a little Jewish girl named Marion who played a game with pebbles to give her hope in a concentration camp.
- Book #38 *Oceans Apart* is the story of a girl from Iowa named Juanita who was a pen pal with Anne Frank before the war.
- Book #52 *A Hidden Life* the story of a young girl hidden on a farm in France during the Nazi occupation.

Other Books *
- *Eva's Story: A Survivor's Tale by the Stepsister of Anne Frank* by Eva Schloss is Eva's memoir of World War II in Holland.
- *The Promise* by Eva Schloss and Barbara Powers tells Eva's inspiring story.
- *After Auschwitz* by Eva Schloss describes her experiences before and after the war.

*Preview all literature for appropriateness for the age group

Technology

Have students write mini-book reports to post on the A BOOK by ME Facebook page where others will read about their opinion of the story. Review with students how to write descriptions and to summarize. Include the theme and lessons learned. Remind students to be respectful in their writings. All posts on the Facebook page will be monitored.

facebook.com / A BOOK by ME

©Never Forget Publishing

Holocaust Series Book 7

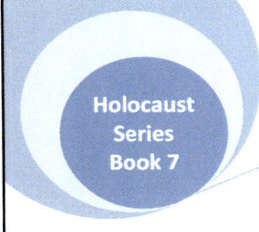

LEARNING STATION

Discussion Questions

1) At the beginning of the story, how are the two families similar? What differences are there between Anne and Eva?

2) Why do you think Anne kept a diary when she was in hiding? Anne writes, "I don't want to have lived in vain like most people. I want to be useful or bring enjoyment to all people, even those I've never met. I want to go on living even after my death!" Did Anne accomplish her dreams? Why or why not?

3) How do you think Otto Frank felt when he found Anne's diary? Otto states, "I began to read slowly, only a few pages each day, more would have been impossible, as I was overwhelmed by painful memories. For me, it was a revelation. There, was revealed a completely different Anne to the child that I had lost. I had no idea of the depths of her thoughts and feelings." Why did Otto choose to publish the diary?

Extended Activities

A) In the introduction of *The Promise*, Eva writes, "I hope through this book you will be moved to share kindness and tolerance with others; appreciate your parents, brothers, sisters and extended family, realizing that your time together is precious; develop your talents to make the world a better place; appreciate the freedom that was won for you through great sacrifice; and value each day." Write an essay about your thoughts on Eva's advice.

B) Eva's brother, Heinz, was an avid painter. Tragically, Heinz perished in the concentration camp, but his talented works of art are cherished by Eva still today. Eva included prints of his paintings in her book *The Promise*. Choose a part of the story that was particularly inspiring to you. Create your own painting to depict that part of the story. Be creative and portray the emotions you think the characters were feeling.

C) The play *And Then They Came for Me: Remembering the World of Anne Frank* by James Still was created in 2005 and has been performed in many countries. Read, perform, or watch the play. It can be found or purchased online.

D) There are many online interviews with Eva posted on YouTube©. Share one with the class. After viewing, have a discussion about what the students learned. Compare the interview with what the students already learned in *Hide & Seek with Evil*. Have the students create their own video in groups. They can share the part of the story that inspired them and what they can do to create a better future.

©Never Forget Publishing

Holocaust Series Book 7

LEARNING STATION

Bullying Definition

According to Olweus Bullying Prevention Program: "A person is bullied when he or she is exposed, repeatedly and over time, to negative actions on the part of one or more other persons, and he or she has difficulty defending himself or herself."

Discussion Questions Relating to Bullying

Do you see examples of bullying in *Hide & Seek with Evil*?
How does this story compare to bullying situations in your own school and community?
What can you do to stop bullying from taking place?

Anti-Bullying Role Playing

Role playing is a way for students to internalize different positions and practice reducing conflict in social situations. Review the possible coping strategies with students. Discuss how to deal with a specific bullying situation. Once the group decides on an appropriate coping strategy(s), students can act it out. Take note that the bully could react in a variety of different ways.

4 ways to describe emotion:
- defenseless
- dominated
- torn apart
- unprotected

Situation: A teenage girl's father gets very angry at her sometimes. When this happens, the girl must hide from him or he hits her. Sometimes she has to hide the bruises from the hitting. The girl is too frightened to tell anyone. What could she do?

Bullying Coping Strategies

- **Avoidance** – Find a way to ignore the bully. Sometimes attention is what the bully wants.
- **Assertiveness** – Sometimes the best way to deal with a bully is to defend yourself by telling them to leave you alone. If you are watching someone else being bullied, stand up for that person.
- **Friendship** – Strength in numbers will sometimes put a bully in his/her place. Find someone who will stand up with you. Be the person who defends a victim of a bully.
- **Education** – Find an adult (teacher, parent, mentor, etc.) to help you educate others about treating all people with respect. If a bully won't back down, get someone with authority to help you stop the situation.

Advice from Eva's Story

Share the stories of the past in hopes of a better future.
Have students discuss and/or write how this advice could be used in their life.

©Never Forget Publishing

Holocaust Series Book 7

LEARNING STATION

Comprehension Questions
Cite evidence from the story text in your answers.

1. What were neighbors Eva and Anne both interested in? _____
_____
_____
_____

2. What freedoms were taken away from the Jews when Nazis invaded Holland? _____
_____
_____
_____

3. Why did the two families choose to live in hiding? _____
_____
_____
_____

4. What happened when the Nazis found people living in the hiding places? _____
_____
_____
_____

5. Who survived living in the concentration camp? _____
_____

6. What did Anne's father, Otto, want to do with Anne's diary after the war? _____
_____
_____
_____

7. Why was Anne's diary published? _____
_____
_____

8. What did you learn from Eva's story? _____
_____
_____
_____

©Never Forget Publishing

Holocaust Series Book 7

LEARNING STATION

Eva is born in 1929 in Vienna, Austria

January 1933 — Hitler became Chancellor of Germany

April 1933 — Nazis organized boycott of Jewish-owned businesses in Germany

August 1934 — Hitler became Führer

June 1935 — Anti-Jewish riots occurred in Poland

September 1935 — Nuremberg "racial laws" took away Jewish citizenship and rights in Germany

March 1936 — More anti-Jewish riots occurred in Poland

July 1936 — Concentration camp constructed near Berlin; 1,000 imprisoned

March 1938 — German troops invaded Austria

November 1938 — Nazis and collaborators burned synagogues (*Kristallnacht*); 30,000 Jewish men arrested and imprisoned in Dachau, Sachsenhausen, Buchenwald and Mauthausen concentration camps

September 1939 — German troops invaded Poland; WWII began in Europe; Britain and France declared war on Germany

October 1939 — Forced deportation of Jews to specific locations

April-June 1940 — German troops occupied Denmark and Norway

June 1940 — German troops occupied Netherlands, Belgium, Luxembourg, and northern France; Southern France was ruled by anti-Semitic government that collaborated with Nazis

Eva's family immigrates to Holland in 1940

Eva becomes friends with Anne Frank, a girl from her neighborhood; In 1942, both families go into hiding

In May 1944, Eva and her family are captured by the Nazis and sent to Auschwitz-Birkenau death camp

Eva and her mother are liberated in January 1945 by the Russians

1940-1945 — Nazis imprisoned Jews in ghettos and camps, and carried out mass killings of six million Jews

December 1941 — Japan bombed Pearl Harbor; U.S. declared war on Japan; Germany and Italy declared war on U.S.

March 1942 — Nazis began deporting Jews from France to camps in Europe, where most perished

June 1944 — British and American troops landed at Normandy, France

August 1944 — Paris liberated by Allies

July 1944-January 1945 — Nazis liquidated ghettos and camps; prisoners evacuated in "death marches"

January – May 1945 — U.S. troops liberated thousands of prisoners in camps

April 1945 — Hitler killed himself in Berlin

May 1945 — German forces surrendered to Allied forces

Anne dies in Bergen-Belsen in March 1945

July 1946 — Polish mob attacked and killed many Jewish survivors

November 1945 — Trials for Nazi leaders began in Nuremberg, Germany

September 1945 — Japan surrendered; WWII officially ended

In May 1945, Eva and her mother are sent back to Amsterdam where they find out Eva's father and brother did not survive; Otto Frank shows them Anne's diary

Eva meets Zvi Schloss in London and they marry in 1952; Eva's mother and Otto Frank marry in 1953; the entire family stays active in Holocaust education and Eva writes her own memoirs

July 1947 — *Exodus 1947* ship carrying 4,500 Jewish refugees sailed for Palestine from southern France; refugees had to return to Displaced Persons (DP) camps

June 1948 — U.S. passed Displaced Persons Act authorizing entry for Jewish refugees to U.S.

1945-1952 — Approximately 80,000 Jewish refugees entered the U.S.

©Never Forget Publishing

*Special thanks to Dr. Marrietta Castle, Professor Emeritus at Western Illinois University, for the development of this timeline
**Curriculum written by Cassie Bowen

A BOOK by ME®
OPERATION WRITE NOW

Deb Bowen, Creator & Director
www.abookbyme.com

"I'm asking ordinary children to do something extraordinary!"

I'm asking ordinary children all over the world to use their talents to share extraordinary stories. Many students write about Holocaust survivors, Righteous Gentiles (non-Jews who risked their lives to save the Jewish people), prison camp liberators and other important stories of World War II. Since this generation is getting older, the time to interview them, write and illustrate their important story is RIGHT NOW!

Some students are deciding to tell important stories about human rights or heroes as well. Check out the website and then decide what interests you. The writer's guidelines are online, and you can register your story once you decide who your subject will be. Also, online you will find a sample of a newspaper article you could use to find a subject in your hometown. Talking to a grandparent, visiting nursing homes, VFW or meeting with a local historian might lead you to a possible story.

All authors / illustrators must be age 18 or under to qualify. All submissions will be given consideration for the A BOOK by ME series, but there is no guarantee the work will be published.

It is my hope you have learned from the book you just read and are interested in reading more work by young authors. It would delight me to know you are inspired to write a book about a subject important to you.

Be careful and watch yourselves closely so you do not forget the things your eyes have seen or let them slip from your heart as long as you live. Teach them to your children and to your children's children.
Deuteronomy 4:9

CYA Calling Youth to Action

1 Kouski's Kids

The War and the Boy shares the remarkable experiences of Roy Kouski, an American soldier in Europe during World War II. Roy's moving story was written by his granddaughter, Brittany Ern. CYA challenges young people who love writing or art to take part in a book project through A BOOK by ME. Make Roy and Brittany proud by becoming one of Kouski's Kids! Check out the writer's guidelines at www.abookbyme.com.

2 Mwalimu's Dream

Mwalimu, a young man from Kenya, came to the USA as a foreign exchange student and went home a young author through A BOOK by ME. Read Mwalimu's Dream to learn how he changed thousands of lives in his village with the gift of clean water. There are still many villages that need wells. CYA hopes your classroom is moved to contribute spare change to dig water wells in undeveloped countries. Your small change can make a big change in someone's life! Take a look at www.wells4wellness.com.

3 Change the World

After World War II, student exchange was created to encourage foreign youth to study in the United States. Exchange provides opportunities to build relationships and share cultures which creates better understanding and mutual respect. People whose countries have been former enemies have become "family" through exchange. Hosts are responsible to provide room and board, love and support. The student provides his/her own spending money and health insurance. Host families are always needed. Contact dbowenexchange@gmail.com to learn more.

Made in the USA
Middletown, DE
14 December 2020